HOW TO
PLOT
ROMANCE
FICTION

HOW TO OUTLINE A ROMANCE NOVEL WHEN YOU ARE AN INTUITIVE WRITER.

NINA HARRINGTON

HOW TO PLOT ROMANCE FICTION

HOW TO OUTLINE YOUR ROMANCE NOVEL WHEN YOU ARE AN INTUITIVE WRITER

Published by NinaHarringtonDigital.

NINAHARRINGTON.COM

FAST-TRACK GUIDES

FOCUSED TRAINING FOR AUTHORS

CONTENTS

INTRODUCTION

ARE YOU AN INTUITIVE ROMANCE WRITER?

Are you an intuitive and organic writer who loves to dive into your writing and discover your story in the process? Does the idea of having to plan your romance novel in advance freeze you, even though you are afraid of getting lost or never finishing a new story?

In the modern publishing world, any successful fiction writer has to become more productive and prolific than ever before. So many of us start a new project bouncing with enthusiasm and energy, excited about our characters, but the brilliant story idea somehow does not come to anything.

We get lost on the way and hit the middle slump and never reach the end.

You know what happens when you hit a difficult part of the writing and you don't think your story is working. You lose momentum. You lose interest. You stop, frustrated and demotivated, put that story to one side, and move on to the next shiny new story idea which is untainted by your sense of frustration and failure.

There are way too many half-written stories that get dragged out every November during NaNoWriMo, only to be put away again.

As a full-time writer, I know how easy it is to get distracted and confused by all of the different story structure elements that need to be in place to create a powerful romance.

I have learnt that you don't have to be.

There is a middle way between meticulous story plotting and full-on organic writing.

EMOTIONAL STORY STRUCTURE

Here is the secret. When you are planning to write a new story, all you need to focus on are your two main characters, and how they are going to change during the course of the romance as a result of the relationship.

You can leverage the power of character arc and emotional conflict to create a simple but powerful emotional story map for the opening scenes of your romance novel.

Not the whole book – just the opening scenes.

As you write your romance, your characters will come to life on the page and reveal their true personalities through what they say and do. That is what will make your story both unique and compelling, and you don't have to plan out the entire plot in advance.

Then, you use what your characters have revealed in these opening scenes to work on the outline for the rest of the book.

Why is emotional story structure so powerful?

Because it all comes from your characters. The hero and the heroine, or other gender couples, who are going to drive your story.

This is not a new technique. On the contrary, screenwriters and commercial advertisement agencies know that every minute of a movie or video clip has to be designed and story-boarded to create a specific emotional response in the viewer.

Not convinced? Look at the sixty-second commercials for Budweiser beer which use Shire Horses and other animals as the main characters. Not a dry eye in the house!

That's the power of emotional story structure. They are not just selling beer; they are selling beer through a story with characters and struggle and hope and love and sacrifice and courage and redemption. And these ads are only **one minute** long.

Just think about what you can do with 50,000 words or more.

Emotional structure gives any writer a solid framework to hang the action and story onto so that the novel or movie is a rollercoaster of an emotional and adrenaline-fuelled ride that readers and audiences will love.

But you will never discover the heart of your story until you can get those characters onto the page and interacting with one another, as they fall in love and reveal their secrets.

That is why the Six-Step story development system I am going to describe in this book is so useful. It is the quickest way that I know to get your characters talking and walking and revealing their inner conflicts and deep desires.

You can use emotional story structure to:

- develop your characters and know them from the start

- create powerful opening scenes in your romance novel

- kick start your imagination in every scene

- sketch out the key signposts from the start to the end of the romance so that you know that you will not get lost on the way, but still have the flexibility to go down interesting sidetracks. You are not held rigidly to a fixed route. Far from it.

Ready to find out more?

"An idea is a point of departure and no more. As soon as you elaborate it, it becomes transformed by thought."
Pablo Picasso

THE INTUITIVE WRITER

I don't know about you, but how many times have you heard that you must create a brilliant synopsis for your novel before a literary agent or submission editor will consider your book?

So, you must either:

- write a first draft of the entire book to discover the story in the process, and then submit the synopsis, or

- outline the book in advance, and risk killing any motivation you have to write it.

Perhaps that is why so many of us convince ourselves that there is no way that we can outline an entire book – that is simply not our process.

I am going to challenge you to rethink that mindset.

Let's begin by killing a few myths that many intuitive writers tell themselves.

MYTH ONE

"Oh, I am totally right-brained. I couldn't possibly plan out anything before I start to write".

Not true.

The idea from the 1970s that all of the creative processes are carried out in the right brain and the logical sequential processes totally in the left has now been debunked and replaced instead by multiple studies which have shown that the brain does have distinct regions, but neural networks across the entire brain work together to build the abstract concept that we call imagination.

The exact detail is still unclear, but it is certainly complex and involved all parts of the brain associated with our higher reasoning.

The human brain is truly remarkable. It only weighs about three pounds and is small enough to hold in your two hands, yet it controls higher functions that control every aspect of our lives. *Including how we read and write.*

Recent studies in neurology have indicated that our ability to speak and interpret spoken sounds is much older than our ability to write.

When we learn to read and write we have to train our minds to associate symbols with sounds and then the sounds to words, but we were born with the capacity to learn a language and communicate through speech.

The language and sequential centres in the left hemisphere of the brain translate the pictures and symbols coming in from the right hemisphere into words and sounds. Those images and pictures are also processed by the limbic system which adds layers of emotional context before they are passed on.

The corpus callosum connects the right and left hemispheres so that signals from the visual cortex can be translated in the parietal lobe into words through a series of complex connections and brain processes that engages all of the higher functioning parts of the brain.

According to psychologist and neuroscientist Stephen Kosslyn, for example, humans tend to be either top-brain or bottom brain centric.

The research demonstrates that the top part of the brain formulates and implements plans, controls movement and revises plans in response to real-life events; at the same time, the bottom part of the brain, which includes the emotional limbic system, categorizes and interprets what we perceive in the world around us so that we can make sense of it.

Both parts of the brain are in constant communication every second of the day, but according to this theory, every one of us has a default operating system that favours using more of the top-brain cortical function or more of the bottom-brain emotional limbic neural networks.

Intuitive writers can relate to this idea that they can harness both neural networks but tend to be guided by sensory details, visuals, memories and emotional experiences associated with the lower part of the brain when they are writing new stories.

The important thing to recognise is that these theories of brain function are all about balance.

There are no hard lines between thinking one way or another, just modes of thinking and processing ideas and information which depends on the context of what you are doing at that moment.

And the best thing? You can seamlessly access different parts of your brain and learn new ways of thinking at any time.

Brain function is constantly changing and building new connections.

MYTH TWO

"I need to spend weeks studying story structure before I can plan my romance novel".

Also not true.

Most professional romance writers that I know are self-taught and came to writing, like you, from a deep passion for reading romance fiction and genre fiction in general.

I was taught to read before I started primary school and have always found the time to read several books a week. Plus we are surrounded by a story in every part of our lives. There is a reason that we love the annual Christmas commercials on TV – supermarkets and stores know the power of a story!

Does that sound familiar?

After decades of enjoying and internalising stories from fiction, TV dramas, movies, advertising copy and animations, it is clear that these story patterns are imprinted into our neural pathways.

We develop intuitive expectations about what we expect to see and read and experience when we read genre fiction, including romance, no matter what subgenre we love the most.

We have a deep inner understanding of story patterns. It is inbuilt and ready to be accessed. They are patterns of action and reaction that are part of every love story.

These are classical story structure forms and they are universal.

So, what happens when we imagine new story ideas?

We are bound to look for existing patterns in our memory. Story patterns that have been imprinted since we first saw a Disney cartoon or comic book, using shapes and images instead of sounds and words.

By the time we reach adulthood we have an internal library of thousands of stories and we intuitively understand the shape of how those stories are formed. Not necessarily from formal training, but from a lifetime of exposure to stories every day of our lives.

This creates a form of mental muscle memory that every writer uses when they have to create words, whether it is a shopping list or an epic ten-volume saga with hundreds of characters.

The net result?

We create an image of what we want to say and this magically emerges at our fingertips in the form of words and those words are combined into sentences.

So why do you have to know all of this?

Because it is clear that many intuitive writers have developed, and can access, neural networks which are geared to creating amazing characters and authentic emotional experiences.

Many writers describe seeing a video clip of their characters in action. These writers can clearly visualise the characters talking and acting and reacting inside a story world and have the ability to take those images and make them come alive on the page.

These writers are discovering the characters and finding out how they are going to react and say, at the same time as the reader. They tend to write from the inside out, using emotions, dialogue, and interactions between the characters to shape the story.

The good news is that these are the perfect skills for any romance writer who wants to create a compelling emotional story structure.

Just as getting to know any person takes more than one meeting, so the more time any writer spends with their characters, the more the characters will reveal themselves on the page.

MYTH THREE

"I only have a small spark of a story idea. There is no way that I could plan out an entire romance novel".

You don't have to plan the whole story.

The goal of emotional story mapping is to give you a kick start to the opening few sequences of scenes in your romance.

It has been my experience that spending time developing your characters in the planning stage will make it possible to set a few signposts further down the road on their journey to their happy ever after or happy for now. But you have to get those characters onto the story world stage and make them come alive so that **they can tell you** how they want to reach the end.

MYTH FOUR

"My creativity, and the inspiration to write this story, will be lost if I try and plan out precisely what is going to happen from start to end".

Not if you focus on the holistic emotional journey the characters will take, rather than a rigid step by step process.

Use your intuitive writing skills to their best advantage, by giving yourself permission to imagine new ideas, using milestones called 'turning points' in the story to guide you on your way.

Romance is a genre that is totally character driven at its core.

Yes, if you are writing romantic suspense or some other subgenre with another plotline, then you have to weave that external plot into the romance so that, depending on your subgenre, your finished story can be anywhere from 50 to 90% romance story.

Editors at publishing houses are desperate for stories with amazing characters that readers will love and remember when they close the last page of the book.

This is what literary agent **David Haviland** has to say: "*My advice to romance writers is to focus on the theme, and the characters' emotional journeys, not just the plot. A common flaw in romance novels is that the plot twists and turns as it should, with obstacles and break-ups, but this is achieved through coincidences and confusion, rather than meaningful conflict between the characters. What is the real friction between the couple that means they may not be able to make the relationship work?*"

This is why professional romance authors spend more time developing characters than anything else. They know that a reader wants to step into the shoes of the heroine and fall in love with the hero and overcome the barriers to their relationship.

How do I know this is true? Because I had to throw what little I knew about writing out of the window and start again from scratch when I decided to write romance fiction.

In 2001 I had a full-time job as a scientist in the pharmaceutical industry.

The work was stressful and demanding but I enjoyed it, had a superb team of people working with me and I was well compensated for all of the efforts.

So why did I give my boss 12 months' notice and walk away in September 2002?

Because I am a writer in my heart and I want to give myself the best chance possible of being a published author before it was too late, and I went to my grave with my stories still burning untold inside of me. Like many people I know, I was squeezing my writing into weekends and family holidays plus 5 am and 9 pm sessions when I could. It wasn't enough. For me, that meant focusing 100% on learning story craft and cramming as much information as I could find on how to write commercial fiction.

Back in 2002, there was little online information available and most of the story craft guides had been written for screenwriters and playwriting. But I was determined to learn and write and then write more. I was so naïve, I thought that it would only take a few years to learn and practice the craft and persuade a publisher to offer me a contract. After all, I had been reading crime, romance, and genre fiction for decades.

I soon discovered that watching back to back episodes of ER and Doctor House and other medical TV dramas will not qualify you to take out someone's appendix.

There was a difference between telling a story and being able to shape that story into the best possible form.

I became obsessed with learning about story craft and was fortunate enough to attend live seminars from Robert McKee, John Sherlock, John Truby, and others.

This was backed up with hundreds of craft books and articles from playwrights, screenwriters, and authors.

My pharmacy degree took three years to complete. When I was offered a contract with Harlequin in September 2008 it was six years after leaving my full-time job.

Since then, I have written 19 romance novels with Harlequin and Carina, self-published romantic suspense, and numerous non-fiction guides for writers, and even won a few romance fiction awards along the way.

Plus there are files of unpublished young adult and thriller manuscripts stashed away out of sight which will probably never be looked at again. And that's okay. Because they served their purpose and helped me to understand how to write compelling fiction that readers and editors love.

After 20 years of working as a full-time writer, I am still a story craft geek, but I can also stand back and see how the craft can be used by every writer.

And the best way to do that is to <u>invest time in pre-planning the opening scenes of your story</u> before you start.

Be ready to acknowledge that you don't know everything about your characters at this point and that is okay. They are going to reveal themselves to you when they are in the writing.

You will be astonished at how little time it will take if you know what works for you. You really can work through your ideas and sketch out a story plan in under an hour.

There is also another factor.

Successful romance authors have to work smarter as well as harder and create more books to generate a working income. If you can focus your time <u>on the start of the story,</u> you can leverage the power of your motivation and energy associated with this story, and your knowledge of story craft, so that you are setting off on the right road right from the start.

Once you have drafted out these first few scenes, then you can use emotional story mapping to develop your hero and heroine and sketch out a story map for the rest of the novel based on what you have learnt in these opening scenes.

This map will be constantly changing and evolving because the characters will dictate how they want to travel to their happy ever after.

Perhaps a deep secret from their past will emerge or a new barrier to the relationship will appear out of the blue. Great! Add that to the storyline and work on the implications as you write the next scenes.

What I am looking for are emotional trigger points and marker points along the emotional story map, which will spark my imagination so that the writing is fun, flows fast and delivers on the promise of the romance.

Let me be clear. I am talking here about starting a new story.

This is a story map. A pattern of steps that will lead you safely down a winding track through a thick forest and allow time for interesting side-tracks.

Emotional story mapping makes it possible to:

- Start a new romance and know that you are going to finish it. No more worry about having nothing to say or that your idea will falter and die after a few chapters.

- Give you a super quick start to writing the first few sequences which will automatically trigger your imagination to create the subsequent scenes and then the ones after that.

- Have confidence that you can dive into the writing and produce words FAST!

- Be completely flexible about how the hero and heroine are going to meet for the first time and then stay locked into a story situation where you can throw rocks at them.

- Accept that you don't know how your characters are going to react to all of these rocks. You can't know until they reveal that to you in the writing.

- Be open to new situations and diversions at any time. These are points on a map, not a fixed route you have to follow.

- Give yourself permission to write a truly rough draft which will not be perfect, but it will reveal what you need to know to edit it when it is complete. Perfectionism can kill if you let it. Think of this draft as an experiment and a piece of fun writing.

- Nobody will see this draft. You can write what you like. Your words will not be examined and judged and criticized. Write it in any tense you want. First person point of view? Great. We love to get inside our character's heads. Switch to multiple third person points of view later on? No problem. Let both the hero and the heroine explain how they are feeling.

- You will know that you will not fail. You are going to follow a story pattern that meets the expectations of anyone coming to enjoy a romance story.

- You are going to enjoy writing this romance because you don't know what is going to happen with these characters as they fall in love. That way it stays fresh and interesting.

- Turn off your internal editor and nasty nagging limiting beliefs long enough to write faster than you thought possible and enjoy it. You can write the scenes out of order or work backwards from the end. It is up to you.

You can still see the road if you look over one shoulder and that gives you the confidence and the freedom to explore as much as you want and learn new things about the characters that are walking by your side.

THE SIX STEP STORY DEVELOPMENT PROCESS

I know that when we set out to write a new story, there is always a mixture of excitement about the new adventure we are about to take, and yet in the back of our minds is a big solid lump of fear.

So what do we do? We might procrastinate and/or dive into the story structure books and training on story craft, and an hour later we start to wonder why we ever thought that we could write a romance in the first place.

There are so many things to think about when it comes to planning a new romance that it is paralysing.

Stop right there!

Story structure tools are super-useful when you come to self-edit and revise your completed manuscript, but they can freeze a lot of writers when they try and use them to outline a new novel.

Some writers do find it helpful to prepare a detailed outline as part of story development, and if that is your process – great! Just be prepared to throw most of your carefully planned outline out of the window when you actually start the writing.

Sorry. But it is a fact.

In my case, extremely detailed story planning with scene lists and pages of character biographies was usually a wonderful way to procrastinate, before I found the courage to get my hero and heroine on the page and find out where they would take me.

So what can we do to pre-plan a new romance story?

The good news is that you don't need advanced story structure when you are planning a romance novel.

We can leverage the power of the one very special aspect of romance fiction which makes it unique; the emotional journey that our hero and heroine will take and how they change as a result of the romance relationship.

Why is this so important?

When you turn the last page of a book, what do you remember most? The thrilling action scenes? The heart-thumping heat of a passionate and sensual love scene that made you sigh out loud?

In my experience what I remember most about a particular book or story are the characters. Something about the hero made me swoon and fall in love with him just as the heroine did.

And what about that heroine? I wanted that girl to be my best friend. She was the equal of the hero and made him work for her love.

There was something about one or more of the characters that I connected with and now I'll love that book forever. Romance fiction is all about the characters.

But that does not mean that you can neglect the plot – the sequence of events that create the strong backbone your wonderful romance is built on.

Let's combine the characters and the plot in one story development process.

HOW TO USE A 6 STEP PROCESS TO GET STARTED

To plan out any new romance story and spark your imagination as quickly as possible, you basically need to do six things.

#Step One: Develop a simple story idea or situation which you can describe in a few sentences.

#Step Two: Focus on ONE main character who will open the story.

#Step Three: Give that main character ONE limiting belief.

#Step Four: Give that main character ONE reason why they are at the end of their tether when the story opens.

#Step Five: Create the ideal hero or heroine who is going to challenge your main character and fall in love with them.

#Step Six: Combine the Story Idea with the Character Idea and get your main character onto the page and inside that story world – then introduce the lover.

Time to use this six-step technique to develop the opening scenes for our new romance story.

STEP ONE. THE PREMISE

Step One: Develop a simple story idea or situation which you can describe in a few sentences.

This is the truly fun part of any story development process.

You are completely free to choose any character type or location or story situation in any romance subgenre or time frame or story world.

This is also the one area where writers spend a huge amount of time, worrying about coming up with a new and fresh story idea that will bring your hero and heroine together.

The truth is, you only need to have a fleeting idea about the story situation or story idea to get started.

There is a reason why romance story tropes like the Cinderella story, Secret Baby, Run-Away Bride or Fake Fiancé, are so successful – they work because these tropes are <u>shortcuts</u> into a story world.

Feel free to take one of those familiar tropes that you enjoy reading and use it as a starting point for <u>your</u> ideas.

Framing your story world.

The goal is this; to create a frame around your characters and the world they inhabit and then set them free to reveal their deep character within the confines of that frame.

The story idea or story situation means that the hero and heroine are trapped inside a situation similar to a closed furnace or crucible, where the pressure and heat inside this crucible will build and build over the story, until they are forced to make a leap of faith and break down the old barriers in order to escape into a long-lasting and loving relationship.

That is what we are trying to capture on paper.

To create that closed crucible we have to frame the story world in a believable way. Think of it like a movie set or the backcloth to a play.

You are creating a magical stage where your characters can come alive.

Brainstorm the 'story idea' then expand and play with your idea and character sketches and situations and develop them into a scenario that is worth exploring.

Play the 'what if' game with those characters and situations then summarize the story idea in one sentence.

This brainstorming process is crucial.

This is the part in the development process where your initial ideas have the chance to run free. This is the most intimate and personal part of the whole story process. And also, the most exciting and invigorating.

In many cases the idea might have been bubbling away inside your head for ages, building up in layers and waiting to be explored, but at this point don't worry if your story idea is not fully developed and the conflicts have not been fully worked out. All you need is a snatch of an idea to spark your imagination.

If you are writing an historical or western romance, for example, the location and story situation may be the very thing that sparks your interest in writing this particular story. Or perhaps you want to explore how modern relationships work in a large city.

One thing we do have to remember is that romance fiction is an escapist form of entertainment for many readers, who pick up a romance novel to be swept away by the uplifting emotional experience. This is not the genre for your hard-hitting prison drama or down-beat story of depression and drug or domestic abuse. That can be a side-plot or backstory element, but not the main storyline.

This also explains the enduring popularity of fantasy locations and romance story themes such as beach weddings, brides, grooms and bridesmaids, winter and summer holiday locations, Mediterranean settings, tropical islands [without the sand flies] and Regency lifestyles.

Please note that I am not suggesting that all romance fiction is fluffy and light. Far from it. Real emotional conflicts that readers can identify with are based on authentic life experiences, good and bad. The darkest moments make the joy of finding love even brighter.

"Maybe you have to know the darkness before you can appreciate the light." – Madeline L'Engle

The key elements of any story world frame should always include:

The physical locations or locations for the story and the time of year.

The time period. Is your story contemporary, time-slip or historical?

The style and voice. For example: witty, suspenseful, heart-wrenching or a fun romp.

The amount of intimate contact you are going to include. From inspirational to erotic romance, the bedroom door can remain firmly closed or left wide open. It is entirely up to you and your story.

The length of book you would like to write. Are you setting out to write a short story, novella, short novel or full-length novel or saga? This does not have to be set in stone. Many authors have started a novella of perhaps 25,000 words and ended with a long-form novel of 80,000 words.

Once you come up with the backdrop setting for your characters, you may need to carry out research to spark your imagination. Small details about a specific location can make a huge difference to how that setting comes alive for the characters.

Many of my own romances are set in locations that I know well, such as London, rural Hampshire, and the Greek Islands. They are contemporary and upbeat with a deep emotional heart.

Example: *Always the Bridesmaid*

The heroine of this book is Amy Edler, 28, sole proprietor of Edler's Bakery in London.

Amy left her corporate job to retrain and open the bakery and is working every hour she can to make it a viable business. Success will validate that decision and show that she can run a business on her own.

Example: *Who's Afraid of the Big Bad Boss.*

The heroine Antonia [Toni] Baldoni has accepted a commission to paint the portrait of the CEO of Elstrom Industries, based in an historic London building. Only the new CEO is not the eminent cartographer Lars Elstrom but his adventurer son Scott, and the last thing he needs is to have his portrait painted.

Example: *My Greek Island Fling.*

When Lexi is offered a job on the Greek island of Paxos, she's can't believe her luck. However, her delight soon gives way to shock when she realizes that she's going to be spending the next couple of weeks with a man who has got good reason to dislike her: The Honourable Mark Belmont.

By working in aspects of the setting into the external conflict of the story idea, you are organically building in an additional sensory level into the novel.

- What does a busy bakery specialising in Austrian pastries smell like?

- How does a cartographer accustomed to working in remote locations cope with the traffic noise and bustle of a large city like London? Do they have a roof-top garden?

- The Ionian islands are famous for their olive trees, pine trees, goats, and cliff-top vistas. Can you create a scene where the two main characters get together overlooking the ocean?

Whatever your setting, once you know the key elements, you can quickly move onto developing your characters.

STEP TWO. ONE CHARACTER

Step Two: Focus on ONE character.

There are going to be two character arcs in any romance since both the heroine and the hero will be transformed a result of the romance relationship.

But at the planning stage, it will pay dividends to focus on ONE character and use that profile as the driver for the start of the story.

I would usually recommend that you spend time developing the character of the heroine.

We want to see the world through her eyes and step into her shoes and fall in love with the hero at the same time as she does.

You can always switch the Point of View character during the self-edit, or when you have completed the first sequence of scenes, but starting with the heroine means that you will get to the heart of your romance story as fast as possible.

- Dive deep into this one character so that you know who she is and how she is likely to act and react when the hero starts challenging her.

- Ask her some questions about her life and what she loves to do in her ordinary world and what she would actually like to do instead.

- Look for photos of actresses or celebrities who you imagine would look like your character, and

- Give her a name and a job or passionate interest. She will have family and friends, somewhere to live and possibly a pet.

- Start asking deep and searching questions about how your character sees the world and how it works, and her place in that world.

The answers will determine the type of decisions that she will make during the course of the story and how her worldview will shift, or arc, from the start to the end of the story because of the romance with the hero.

These are designed as kick-off questions and there are bound to be lots more that are specific to your character and your book and the context of that book. The detailed psychology of this character may not emerge until you have written several chapters, and that's absolutely fine.

One thing however is crucial to the success of your romance fiction. The profile you create for your characters has to be credible and understandable.

Example story situation: WHAT IF?

Imagine that you are writing a contemporary romantic comedy novel where your heroine lives in a large modern cosmopolitan city where she specialises in arranging themed weddings.

If your heroine has such an obsession with her appearance that she has spent all of her money on luxury goods and shoes, and is broke when the story opens, then you could use this for comedic value to make the reader sympathise with her situation when she has to go and arrange a cowboy themed wedding at a ranch.

But what if it turns out that actually, this silly girl is a jilted bride?

Her fiancé ran off with her maid of honour the night before the wedding only a few months earlier, leaving her to clear up the mayhem and financial disaster of the wedding she had planned and paid for. She has had no time to grieve or come to terms with the trauma of that event.

Her reluctance to start a new trusting relationship with the best man at the cowboy wedding suddenly becomes more credible.

The internal barriers that the heroine has created to having any kind of relationship must be there from the start. Then you can add on the extra barriers to her falling for the lovely hero who you are going to drop into her life.

But you have to start with a solid idea of what her internal conflict is. This is where the concept of a *Limiting Belief* becomes important.

> ## "Character is plot, plot is character."
> ### F. Scott Fitzgerald

STEP THREE. ONE LIMITING BELIEF

Step Three: Give your heroine ONE limiting belief.

This girl will probably have more baggage than Victoria Beckham launching a new fashion collection. But do you know what? You don't need to know all of this when you are planning a new novel.

The early life experiences of that character have led to your heroine's inherent system of beliefs about how the world works and her place in that world. This creates powerful emotional and internal conflicts.

What you <u>do</u> need is some sense of how your heroine is going to change or *arc* over the course of the story.

HOW TO USE CHARACTER ARCS TO BUILD A ROMANCE STORY

There are four overarching components of any piece of romance fiction, irrespective of the length.

- The Romance Story. How the romance relationship builds.

- The Character Arc of the Heroine over the course of the story.

- The Character Arc of the Hero over the course of the story.

- The Plot. The external story situation that will bring the hero and heroine together, even if they are battling against one another for the same prize. In most cases, this acts as the spine for the story.

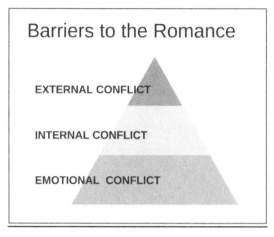

In the opening scenes, we are introduced to the hero and heroine in their ordinary life, with all of the limiting beliefs and behaviours that they have created to protect themselves.

WHAT DO I MEAN BY THE TERM *LIMITING BELIEF?*

Each of us lives within and operates out of a complex set of beliefs and behaviours that define us and our interaction with the world in which we live. Our beliefs are linked to our feelings of self-worth and self-esteem and how we believe other people in the world see us.

A limiting belief is a powerful and deep-seated belief that we are not capable of doing something, or being someone, or feeling something. This belief holds us back from achieving what we are capable of.

In most cases, these limiting beliefs are based on our personal past experiences and lessons learnt dealing with people and situations before the story begins.

Example Story Idea. Our heroine works for a brand management company that has a new musical Rockstar client.

As a teenage student, she was repeatedly ridiculed and told at school and at home that she did not have any musical talent and she was wasting her time trying to become a singer. Over time she came to believe this as fact. She suppressed her passion for music and went on to do other things.

She now believes that she has no musical talent. This will be challenged by the hero Rockstar client she has to work with.

The reader wants to see that character transformed from the start to the end of the book because of her relationship and the difficult choices she has to make under pressure, so you have to show on the page how much of a journey that person is going to have to make and how much they will resist the pain of having to face their fears.

Show her at her lowest point when the story opens.

The bigger the fear, the greater the satisfaction for the reader!

By the end of the book, the hero and heroine have to learn how to break through those limiting beliefs. They must move from living in a state of fear to living courageously, as a direct result of the romance relationship expressed on the page of this novel.

These controlling and sometimes limiting beliefs set the rules the character uses to make decisions in their life, especially when it comes to protecting themselves from emotional pain or loss.

- **What is her short term goal when the story starts?** An external goal with a clear endpoint linked to a chance to achieve her longing or need. She has to do this to make a big change in his life.

- **What are the stakes?** What happens if she does not achieve this goal?

- **Why now?**

- **What is her long term goal**, her longing, that deeply held desire which she has not found the courage to go after yet?

- **What is her need?** The thing that is missing in her life which will make it complete?

- **What is her wound?** The unhealing source of continuing pain. This has led to the identity mask that they show to the world, which will be chipped away during the story journey.

- **What is her ONE core belief about the way the world works** - the universal code she lives by?

- **And what is the deep fear that is linked to this belief?** What would destroy them/wound them again/cause them pain again?

- **How does this ONE Internal Conflict** create the RELATIONSHIP BARRIER?

As the relationship develops, this one powerful belief will be challenged and the damaging and limiting elements overcome with the help of the other romance character, who in turn has their own set of controlling beliefs.

In the opening chapters, the reader will only know how the character reacts to the challenges they are hit with, but it is crucial that you know the deep-seated root cause of these beliefs which are the foundation for the character's internal conflicts.

In a romance, we are mainly concerned with the emotional internal conflicts, but there could be several layers to these beliefs which will be revealed at the crisis key decision points in the story.

That starts with understanding that ONE core belief that controls how the heroine sees the world.

WORKED EXAMPLE OF CHARACTER ARC IN ACTION

"Who's Afraid of the Big Bad Boss" by Harlequin Mills and Boon Modern Tempted.

Story Summary

Antonia [Toni] Baldoni has accepted a commission to paint the portrait of the CEO of Elstrom Industries. Toni needs the money to help pay for her younger sister's gap year with something left for the university fees. Toni has taken care of her sister since their parent's death.

Only the new CEO is not the eminent cartographer Lars Elstrom but his adventurer son Scott. Scott might be the last of the line, but he is not going to let 200 years of heritage go down without a fight. And Toni might just be the girl he needs to help him do that.

The Themes of the Story are Family Loyalty and Letting go of the past.

Character Development of the Heroine.

Heroine is Antonia Baldoni [Toni].

Opening Image. Toni is in the living room of a smart London townhouse trying on lingerie and flicking a feather whip at her sister

Amy and about a dozen of her friends who organised a fun lingerie birthday party.

Heroine in her ordinary world

Toni is house-sitting in the smart London house owned by Fiona Elstrom. Fiona was the one who got in contact and asked Toni to paint a portrait of her father, the CEO of Elstrom Industries.

The Baldoni family have painted the last 4 generations of Elstroms. Very traditional. And it is what Fiona's father wants before he leaves the company for good.

Fiona suggested that she could use the empty London house rent free for a few weeks. Toni plans to rent out her cottage while her sister is away and is renovating it and decorating it.

Toni is working for an independent UK TV company that specialise in making documentaries and hugely popular TV shows such as the BestChef series which has gone global, and Toni is going to be travelling from now on.

Reveal: When Toni mentioned that is her birthday AND the first anniversary of breaking up with her cheating boyfriend, then the girls on the show insisted that they hold a party for her to mark the occasion. Toni's younger sister Amy thought this was a great idea and arranged the whole thing while she was at work.

Now Toni is on holiday for 2 weeks on a commission for a portrait of businessman Lars Elstrom.

Amy is just about to go on a gap year trip starting in South America. Toni is nervous and proud of her little sister.

What is her short term goal when the story starts? An external goal with a clear endpoint linked to a chance to achieve her longing or need. She has to do this to make a big change in his life.

To survive this embarrassing lingerie party that her sister Amy and her pals set up for her and then get ready to paint the portrait of businessman Lars Elstrom.

Toni needs the money for her sister. After this portrait, Toni is going to work full time for the TV company so this could be the last portrait that she ever paints.

What are the stakes? What happens is she does not achieve this goal?

This portrait is a life saver. If she does not get paid, she will need to take a second job or move to a cheaper area to pay the bills and help Amy. But there is also a personal reason.

She wants to prove to herself that she can do this and carry on the family heritage of portrait painting.

Why now?

Amy is about to leave on her gap year – all grown up and leaving home and Toni can start looking to her own needs and old dreams. Toni has decided to rent out the cottage that they inherited and move into somewhere smaller. Big upheaval for them both.

What is her long term goal, her longing, that deeply held desire which she has not found the courage to go after yet?

Toni would love to earn a living painting portraits, but she knows how hard it is to gain a reputation and does not have the finance to make it happen. Her sister has to come first.

What is her need? The thing that is missing in her life which will make it complete.

Toni needs to know that she is perfect the way she is – she has always felt broken and unworthy and second best. Still feels lost and shaken even after a year after the boyfriend left her. She is 25 and was with Alan for 18 months.

What is her wound? The unhealing source of continuing pain.

The sudden death of her artist parents when she was 18 and her sister Amy was 12. Toni had to become the breadwinner and gave up her training in fine art to work in commercial photography to pay the bills and take care of Amy.

This has led to the identity mask that they show to the world, which will be chipped away during the story journey.

On the surface, Toni seems confident and clever and bursting with energy and enthusiasm. Can do anything. The real Toni is scared. New start. New home.

She has not felt like painting since the breakup which rocked her.

She is not brave enough to face new challenges and push the boundaries at this point.

What is her ONE powerful core belief about the way the world works- the universal code she lives by?

People will reject you and let you down if you open your heart. So, do not love them and let them in.

What is the deep fear that is linked to this belief? What would destroy them/wound them again/cause them pain again?

She feels unworthy of love and has suffered lots of rejection of all kinds in her life.

She fears giving her heart only to have it rejected again – leaving her abandoned.

How does this Internal Conflict create the RELATIONSHIP BARRIER?

Toni will fight her attraction to Scott because she has been there before and it is too painful when he leaves and he will leave, that is obvious.

What is the one overpowering dilemma in this story? And who does it belong to?

The dilemma is the choice between staying in the past or moving forward to danger, and it belongs to Toni who is the person who changes most.

I hope that you can see that at this point in the pre-writing process, jotting down answers to these type of questions can help you dive deep into the character of your heroine – and then your hero – fast!

You only need to note down a few words for each question before you start writing but having a sketch idea of who your heroine is will get you onto the page quicker.

You know how this girl will react when she is faced with external and internal challenges and what the likely barriers to the romance could be when she meets the hero.

Will her belief system change and develop?

Of course.

You may well discover a completely new and more devastating backstory during the writing. And that is how it should work when you allow the character to reveal themselves to you.

STEP FOUR. ONE CONFLICT

Step Four: Give her ONE reason why she is at the end of her tether when the story opens.

Just ONE. This is usually the ONE thing that she wants at that moment but feels frustrated that she cannot achieve.

Both the hero and the heroine must have a powerful and all-consuming short term goal when the story opens which is easy to understand and for the reader to relate to.

It is usually an external goal, in contrast to the one limiting belief that you have already worked on.

Link this desire to the story desire line idea/premise to make the character come alive in that story situation. We are going to attack this character with all kinds of trouble and blocks so that they reveal who they are under pressure.

The stakes for reaching that goal must be set high to make the reader care about whether they achieve it or not.

In most cases, it is something deeply personal and linked to family or friends, but it can be as fundamental as the heroine winning the promotion that she had been working for, buying her dream home, or saving the family firm.

Whatever that goal is, that external conflict has to:

- drive the conflict in the opening scenes

- act as a mechanism for bringing the heroine and the hero together in some way

- fuel the action and reaction and decisions that our heroine will take.

Don't worry about whether this text will end up in your final manuscript or not. This is playtime using free writing as an experiment to get the "feel" of whether this character is someone you like and want to spend time with for the next few weeks or months.

If they are? Great. Stay with them after you have completed the opening sequence of scenes and use their emotional conflict to sketch out the rest of the story.

But if you are not interested in writing about this person, then this is the time to find out. Scratch that idea and go back to Step Two and redevelop your character.

Stakes.

What would happen if the heroine failed to achieve their goal?

Why should we care?

This is a crucial element in creating believable character motivation.

How? *By making the character sympathetic and empathetic.*

The reader feels sympathy for their situation and empathises with their need to achieve their goal because it could happen to us. This creates that gut emotional appeal that grabs you as a reader and makes the story feel personal.

We need the reader to identify with the character and care about the outcome of the story. So, it pays to make the character suffer and set them against overwhelming blocks to achieving their goal.

Then you can develop the external conflicts between the hero and heroine based on the story situation and their individual desires and goals. The external conflict is the obvious "on the surface" reason why the hero and heroine could never be together. They want different things and might come from completely different social or economic backgrounds.

The Story Desire Line is the question that will be answered by the end of the story.

Example: Jilted Bride Wedding Planner Idea

If the heroine is both a wedding planner and a jilted bride, then she is going to have some serious issues still believing in marriage and what she is doing. But she is still paying off the bills for her abandoned wedding, and this is the only job she knows. That is why she agreed to organise a cowboy wedding at short notice.

Her short term goal is to make the wedding a success and generate some income.

What if? The hero is the best man at this cowboy wedding. He has his own reasons for not wanting to be there and no wedding date. Perhaps he is divorced or just come through a breakup from a long relationship. But he does believe in marriage and takes it seriously.

His short term goal is to make sure that his brother's wedding is as perfect as possible.

Example: Always the Bridesmaid

Amy Edler is a baker who is making her best friend's wedding cake and she has not heard from the wedding planner in weeks. She does not want to worry her friend who is overseas, but time is running out.

Amy is determined to make her friend's wedding a success and build her business as a celebrity wedding cake designer.

Example: Who's Afraid of the Big Bad Boss.

Toni Baldoni wants to survive this embarrassing lingerie party that her sister and her pals set up for her and then get ready to paint the portrait of a company CEO. Toni needs the money for her sister's education, but the commission is touched with sadness.

After this portrait, Toni is going to work full time for the TV Company so this could be the last portrait that she ever paints, ending her family's long history as portrait painters. Marking the start of her new life. So, the sooner she gets the work done the better!

We are not Writing Fiction –
We are Creating an Emotional
Experience for the Reader

STEP FIVE. THE HERO

Step Five: Create the ideal hero who is going to challenge your heroine and fall in love with them. Link this hero to the story idea so that their relationship is locked into the external plot at the same time.

The main character is going to be the person who has to make the biggest character change in the story. Once you have a powerful limiting belief for your main character, you can think about the other character in this romance, the lover.

This is broad strokes characterisation at this stage and the goal is to have just enough to have these two characters off the page and onto the story stage, acting and reacting and talking about what matters to them.

Consider how you are going to introduce the hero.

The stronger the heroine, then the stronger the hero should be. He has to be a good match and equal to her in every way, with the qualities she needs in her life at that moment.

If she had been betrayed in the past, then he has to show that he is loyal and honest and worthy of her trust. And not just once.

In these opening scenes, he has to come onto the page and be totally authentic and honest from the start. No pretence. One lie here and unless it is powerfully motivated then the heroine will never trust him.

So, think of a couple of ways in which a hero would attack that internal conflict that the heroine is wearing as her armour.

WORKED EXAMPLE OF CHARACTER ARC FOR THE HERO IN ACTION

"Who's Afraid of the Big Bad Boss" by Harlequin Mills and Boon Modern Tempted.

Character Development of the Hero, Scott.

The hero is Scott Elstrom.

Opening Image. Scott is racing alone across frozen sea ice in Alaska on a dog sled. Show that he is a take-charge sort of man. Rugged outdoor type.

Hero's Ordinary World.

Scott is a mapmaker for an ecological survey in Alaska.

What is his short-term goal when the story starts?

An external goal with a clear endpoint linked to a chance to achieve his longing or need – he has to do this to make a big change in his life.

To get back to the base station and transport back to London. His father had been taken ill and his sister needs him to get back to London and help with their father and the company.

What are the stakes? What happens if he does not achieve this goal?

The company will go to the wall – he had no idea how ill his father was and how bad things had become.

Why now?

Going back to London was going to happen someday but he had worked for months on this project in Alaska and was not expecting to go back so soon. Scott is ready to accept his inheritance and a new relationship even if he does not know it.

What is his long-term goal – his longing- that deeply held desire which he has not found the courage to go after yet.

To prove to his father that he is not a failure and can do the job he needs him to do – take over the struggling family business and make a difference.

What is his need? The thing that is missing in his life which will make it complete.

Scott needs someone to share his life with and accept him for who he is, and not for who he is expected to be.

What is his wound? The unhealing source of continuing pain.

His divorce 2 years earlier. He left the business and London and took off doing what he loves most – exploration and adventure in hard places. By the end of the story, Scott will have accepted the end of that relationship and be ready to start again with Toni.

This has led to the identity mask that they show to the world – which will be chipped away during the story journey.

Take charge, nothing is too difficult, action man who excels in extreme environments. Clever scientist but a bit of a loner. Keeps his personal life to himself.

What is his core belief about the way the world works- the universal code he lives by?

You have to live your own life because trying to fit into someone else's ideas only leads to disaster.

And what is the deep fear that is linked to this belief? What would destroy them/ cause them pain again?

Scott and his sister saw the effects of their parent's divorce– it broke their mother. And now he is divorced. Not what he wanted and very painful. Not going to take that risk again without being very sure that he can trust a girl to be faithful to him.

How does this Internal Conflict create the RELATIONSHIP BARRIER?

The last thing Scott wants to do is date a spoilt city girl who has no clue about the life he leads in the field and expects him to change his life for her.

What draws the Hero and Heroine together?

Scott has come back to London out of loyalty to his heritage and his family. Part of that loyalty is going ahead to try and save the company, but having his portrait painted is a joke, seeing that the business is about to fold.

Toni is painting this portrait out of loyalty to her heritage and the family obsession with painting. She has no formal training but is a natural talent.

Why does she really want to paint? The real reason stems directly from Toni's **emotional conflicts and the character arc that I am setting up.**

She is determined to prove her family wrong. She is worthy of being considered a talented member of the Baldoni artist family.

Toni is attracted to Scott because he values the past. It is all around him in the historic building where the company began 200 years earlier.

Scott is attracted to Toni because she is different. She does not try to impress him, she simply tells him what she sees, the truth.

What will keep the Hero and Heroine apart?

What obstacles are they going to have on the journey to find love?

Their external conflicts.

Toni is determined to go ahead and paint this picture. She has taken the 50% deposit from Fiona and used the cash to pay for Amy's gap year trip.

Scott does not want to waste time. He cannot afford to spend hours sitting in one place when he has a business to save.

Their Internal conflicts.

Scott is still reeling from his divorce.

Toni does not want to go through rejection again. She feels unworthy of love, but she does not need a man like Scott reminding her.

Will Toni persuade Scott to have his portrait painted and save the family business at the same time?

How can they fall in love along the way?

Now you can plan out the crucial opening scenes of your romance novel using these character arcs to drive the transformation, even though you haven't written a word of the novel!

STEP SIX. STORY AND CHARACTERS GET TOGETHER

Step Six: Combine the Story Idea with the Character Ideas for your Heroine in that story world, then introduce the Hero.

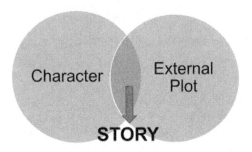

The plot is built up by the actions that the characters take under pressure.

Start by building a strong sense of who your main characters are. Then add a dilemma, challenge, or conflict. Their responses, actions and decisions will automatically generate your plot.

THEN you can start shaping those reactions into the best form possible for this story.

Character is Revealed by their actions and reactions and decisions in response to challenges introduced by the External Plot situation.

In turn, The Plot is driven by those reactions and decisions in a series of Scenes and Sequels to those scenes where the decision taken at the end of one scene triggers the response to that action in the opening of the next scene.

In this six-step technique, we are going to be working on the opening scenes of the romance.

To effectively create scenes that will hook your readers from the first page, I would recommend spending time learning the basic elements of classical story structure and story craft.

Why? If you understand what the first few chapters have to achieve within the framework of the overall novel, it makes it a lot easier to focus on these opening scenes that make up Act One of the romance novel.

WHERE DO WE BEGIN?

Modern readers expect to be entertained. There are certain storytelling conventions that have become engrained into our minds through every book that we have ever read, and every play, radio drama, TV show or movie that we have ever seen, from animated cartoons to the latest special effects blockbuster.

You may not even be aware of these subconscious expectations because they are totally enmeshed in our brains, but as readers we expect the story to be developed in a certain pattern and sequence of events and revelations and stages.

All the reader cares about is the emotional experience that you have created for them on the page.

Now is the time to start working on the story structure of that working draft so that you can take your hero and heroine on an emotional journey to love, which demonstrates the full potential of your characters and the story situation that you have created.

This means that your first draft of the novel needs to have several key dramatic twists or reveals, called "turning points", when the story shifts or something is revealed, and the stakes increase. In this way, the story moves on and builds, and there are no sagging middles but a controlled pace.

The best analysis of story structure comes from screenwriters. Their job is to choreograph and control the emotions of the audience who is watching the movie at every minute.

STORY STRUCTURE MAGIC FOR ROMANCE FICTION.

What is the structure of genre fiction and how can you develop the right structure for your story?

I've spent years studying story craft, plus, as a published romance author with Mills and Boon and HarperCollins, I have worked with several terrific editors who have shared with me in-depth information about story structure, character development and how to write compelling romance fiction. This is gold!

I learnt how to combine story craft with romance specific story structure to create award-winning romance fiction.

In this section, I am going to share with you some of the deep story structure craft that I have learnt as a full-time writer.

And more importantly, **how you can use that story structure to take your story from good to great.**

Please note that I make no apologies for the fact that I am a scientist so there will be lots of tables, charts, and plans and lists. That is how my scientist's brain works, but it may not be your process and that's totally cool.

These ideas are not designed to intimidate you. *Far from it.* My goal is to give you a solid framework for any romance that you can adapt, use, take which parts make sense and then apply it to your draft.

Imagine that you are building a house.

You start at the bottom with the foundations, the groundwork, the floor layout, and the underpinnings of the building. Then the building work begins for an office block, residential home, or a retail store – whatever your plan dictates.

Story structure is the foundation which underpins all of your work.

On top of those foundations, you can build any kind of fresh and new story you like, of any length and in any romance subgenre. The foundations of the story stay the same. The story you build on those foundations is your creative genius - but you need that structure to support the story. Does that make sense? I hope so.

The story and characters may sound great as an idea but without structure, you will end up sliding down the side of the mountain.

USING SCREENWRITING STORY CRAFT

Screenwriting Techniques and Fiction

The good news is that the same story structure techniques used by screenwriters can be applied to fiction. And especially commercial genre fiction such as romance.

Why? Because the goal of a screenwriter is precisely the same as a novelist: to choreograph and control the emotions of the audience who is watching the movie at every minute.

In classical story structure, a novel is made up of sequences of scenes that build into Four Acts. Screenwriters sometimes combine acts 2 and 3 to create a Three Act structure, but the elements are the same.

Act One	Act Two	Act Three	Act Four
Show the hero and heroine in their ordinary life, with the limiting beliefs they have created to protect themselves.	This is the falling in love stage! The hero and heroine start to see that their lives can be different – if they let go of their old beliefs.	Commitment to the other person leading to increased vulnerability, but then something happens which challenges them again and they revert to the old fears.	They take a leap of faith and do what they have always wanted to do, because of the romance relationship.

CONFLICT CHART

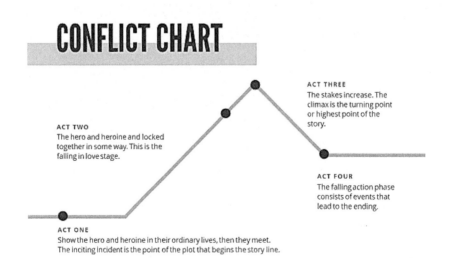

ACT TWO
The hero and heroine and locked together in some way. This is the falling in love stage.

ACT THREE
The stakes increase. The climax is the turning point or highest point of the story.

ACT FOUR
The falling action phase consists of events that lead to the ending.

ACT ONE
Show the hero and heroine in their ordinary lives, then they meet. The inciting incident is the point of the plot that begins the story line.

Clearly, the number of scenes in each sequence will depend on the length of your work.

In classical story structure, scenes are collected into Sequences of scenes where there is a start, middle and end to each Scene Sequence. Every Sequence ends with a turning point that hooks onto the next Scene Sequence.

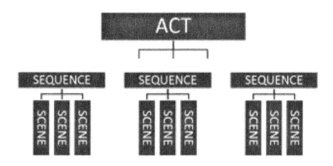

If you are writing a long novel, it could be 3 or 4 sequences per Act, while a short story may only have 1 sequence broken into small scenes.

In a properly structured novel, the story consists of six basic stages, which are defined by five key turning points in the plot. Not only are these turning points always the same; they always occupy the same positions in the story.

STORY TURNING POINTS

Think of these story turning points as tent poles, holding up the rest of the story as the conflict increases. If the tent poles are all on one side of the tent, then the whole thing is completely unbalanced and will collapse.

These five turning point technique helps us set milestones on the journey your characters are taking.

Most importantly, the Four Act structure makes sure that your story will meet the expectations of your readers who want to see the characters battle against the odds and make the wrong choices before they can be together.

THE FOUR ACT, EIGHT-SEQUENCE STORY PLAN

THE FOUR ACT, EIGHT-SEQUENCE STORY PLAN

Here is how it works for, let's say, a 60,000 word first draft of a romance novel.

There eight sequences of scenes with two sequences for each of the four acts.

Act One

Sequence 1. Introduce and establish your hero and heroine in their ordinary world.

Hook the reader with interesting characters. Build sympathy and empathy by showing that they are lacking something. They come onto the stage with their own needs and wants and expectations for the future.

By the end of the first sequence, the reader should know the external conflict of both characters and the internal conflict – what is missing in the life/psychology of the protagonist which the other person will fulfil. This is the start of their character arcs.

This sequence ends with a Plot Point or Turning Point #1, called the **Inciting Incident.** Something unusual happens in this ordinary world which completely turns their world around.

About 10% to 15% of the way through the book.

Sequence 2. Our hero and heroine have to react to this Inciting Incident and new situation.

They don't want to change, and they are going to resist moving out of their established lives, but something pushes them to commit to change and try something new.

This is linked to their motivation and needs at this point, but one thing is clear. From now on their lives will be very different.

They have a new specific objective to achieve and decide to go for it.

This is the external plot that brings the hero and heroine together and forces them to stay locked together. The romance begins!

This is **Turning Point#2**. About 25% of the way through the book.

The rest of your story builds out from this Turning Point.

These are the opening two sequences of scenes that you are going to focus on in the Six-Step Story Development Process

Then build on what your characters have revealed to sketch out notes for Act Two, then Acts Three and Four.

Act Two

This is the falling in love stage of the book.

Sequence 3. connection and communication.

The hero and heroine are working together on a joint project or being forced to communicate and interact with one another in some way.

They are still relying on their old self-protection mechanisms but start to see another side of the person as they are forced to work together and communicate.

Attraction increases. She beings to notice more about him, how he talks, the tones he uses, the words he uses and how he acts.

Sequence 3 ends in a pinch point where something changes in their relationship.

Sequence 4. Recognition and communication.

Slowly they start to re-evaluate one another and communicate like human beings. Building acceptance and trust as they enjoy being with the other person.

Sequence 4 ends with a major shift in the external plot and the relationship which locks the hero and heroine together in a powerful way. This could be a sexual, close, intimate, or personal moment, but it has to be a fundamental shift that changes the entire direction of the story.

This is Turning Point#3, at about the halfway point through the book. This is also known as the Midpoint of No Return. They cannot go back from this point. Everything else that follows pivots on this midpoint scene right in the middle of the book.

Act Three

Sequence 5. The Stakes Increase.

After the midpoint, the stakes increase at several levels for both hero and heroine. The relationship becomes threatened by complications and issues.

Their limiting beliefs and fears are overcome by deep connection. They step outside of their comfort zone and start to disclose and share their life with the other person.

Usually, there is intimacy and passion for one another, leading to a strong trusting bond between them, locking them even closer together.

The heroine [or the hero] is trusting enough to share her background "ghost" and the cause of her inner conflict with the hero. He responds tenderly to the revelation with warmth and understanding. Sincere bonding. Intimacy and sensitivity. Protection.

Sequence 5 ends in a pinch point where something changes in their relationship at around the 62 to 65% point in the book.

Sequence 6. Stakes and problems ramp up as the external and internal conflict increases as their passion develops.

They have grown mutually dependent on one another and feel a natural bond between them. Both hero and heroine have moved away from their limiting beliefs and into a trusting growth state because of their relationship.

The hero [or the heroine] shares his source of pain and internal conflict in a major revelation scene.

Then something happens. Some major revelation threatens their relationship, usually through the external conflict, which directly challenges the internal conflict and fears of one of them.

It could be linked to the revelations about the character's backstory, or a betrayal of their trust or self-worth, for example where the other person had been keeping the whole truth hidden. But this is a major set-back.

One of them steps away from the relationship and retreats back into the old self-protective mode.

Sequence 6 ends with Turning Point#4, Major Setback, at about the 75% point through the book.

This is also known as the Dark Night of the Soul or the Black Moment and is a compulsory plot point in any romance.

Act Four

Sequence 7. Everything they have gained in the story and the entire relationship seems at risk. They are under attack.

All of their fears about being vulnerable are back in place. Their old belief systems threaten to destroy this relationship.

Hero and heroine have to regroup and work out what to do next in the final push to build a relationship, using the new strengths and lessons they have learnt in their character growth. They are not the same person they were when the story began.

They have to take a remarkable leap of faith in the other person.

Sequence 7 ends in Turning Point#5. The Climax decision. Do or die. Commit, compromise or walk away.

Sequence 8. Sequence 8 is the aftermath and resolution of the Climax decision as the hero and heroine commit to one another and find a life together.

Either the hero or the heroine, and ideally both, has a self-revelation that drives them to be the person who represents their true self.

They have to show how they have grown, overcome the obstacles and conquered their old beliefs.

They earned their happiness and this is it.

PLOTTING THE OPENING SCENES

Nora Roberts calls her first rough draft of any new story the "discovery draft".

"I don't outline--it's just not my process. I have a basic situation, a cast of characters, and a canvas or setting...If my characters don't take over at some point, I'm not doing my job--which is to make them real for me so they'll be real, and compelling, for the reader. It's their story, so they need to drive the train."

Every writer I have spoken to uses a different process, which can change depending on the sort of story they are writing and how close they are to deadline. But most of us spend some time free thinking and free writing and playing with ideas as part of the story development process.

MIND MAPPING AND BRAINSTORMING

This is meant to be a visual representation of every thought and idea you have inside your head about the characters and the story idea and setting.

If you have not worked through the six-step process in the earlier chapters, now is the time to go back and start taking notes as you work through each of the six steps.

Get everything down onto paper. Forget about the rules and use as many colours as you like and as many pieces of paper or a whiteboard and just go for it and have fun.

There is mind mapping software but where is the freedom in that? A hand-drawn mind map is quick, easy, and cathartic all in one, and it is free and super quick.

Simply start with the main story idea or the main character and just fill in the side branches of the tree and see where it takes you.

WHAT SPARKS YOUR IMAGINATION?

It might only be a picture of a face from a magazine or online. Or a mental snippet of a movie scene or dream where the hero and heroine are chatting.

Anything at all. Explore every option you can think of. Nobody is watching. This is only for you.

Alien love trios?

The hero is a hitman, and your heroine is his next target?

The birdwatcher and the lumberjack?

Sometimes you have only an idea or a mental image for a situation or a scene or two. For example, a picture of a middle-aged woman walking along the Seine in Paris in winter, holding a bunch of violets in her gloved hands. Or a single photograph of a man's face.

In most cases that spark of inspiration for a story comes with the characters as Nora Roberts does, and our job is to create a cast of people who are going to come alive in this story.

Go wild. And if you suddenly have another idea – simply start another mind map and find out where the map will lead you.

Stand back and look at the mind map and decide on which adventure is going to be the most interesting and challenging for the characters and the readers.

Select one storyline which will put the hero and heroine under pressure and make them change because of the romance relationship.

The characters. Because this is a romance story we are going to focus on the characters and the conflict between them and how this is overcome because of the romance, but at a very high level.

At the end of the six-step process, all we want to see is a very high level and objective plan of the main points, so you are looking out for the major turning points where something can happen or is revealed which makes the characters react and shift and change.

COMPILE A SIMPLE OUTLINE

Write down a simple list of everything that you imagine could happen at the start of your story.

This is how you are going to dive into the story world and start swimming in the opening sequence of scenes.

Bullet points are fine at this stage. What you are looking for is a series of events and character changes which are like stepping-stones on the map from the start to the end.

By keeping the outline at a fairly high level you are giving yourself enough freedom to take a shortcut or spend an afternoon at the beach, but you know that you can easily get back on track when your characters are ready.

A story map is a starting point for an exciting journey into the unknown.

By using an emotional map of the opening sequence of scenes in a story I know that I have set down a welcome mat for the characters which will allow them to take over but still guide them on a journey that will lead to a satisfying ending.

The first draft is always going to be for yourself. Nobody else is going to read it or critique it unless you want them to. That's why it doesn't matter that it is the absolute bare bones of your final story which needs fleshing out, or, in my case overwritten with way too much detail, which will need pruning back.

You can write the scenes out of order when the idea hits you, capture a snatch of dialogue that slips into your head and generally get this first rough draft down any way you like.

I believe that most intuitive authors have a deep understanding of story structure so deeply ingrained into their creative process that they instinctively understand what they need to do to create a solid first draft without writing down an outline. They have the whole story in their heads and can get into onto the page fast.

To be clear; I am talking here about the initial story development part of the writing.

When it comes to revision I turn into a story structure fiend, but not here.

Here I am looking for characters who I want to spend time with for the next few weeks.

I want to let them tell me their story and reveal who they are under the pressure of a romance and the story situation.

This is playtime. You set light to your creativity and let it rocket into the sky.

Every single writer is different and what works for me might not work for you. In my process, I start with the opening chapters and work from front to back.

Reminder. We have four acts with two sequences of scenes per act. This is for a 60,000-word novel so the number of scenes in your story could be very different, but the basic framework still applies.

Reminder - Act One has two sequences of scenes in a typical novel-length romance.

Act One. Sequence One. From page one to the Inciting Incident.

The opening scenes have to work very hard to hook your reader.

Introduce and establish your heroine in their ordinary world.

Normally the point of view [POV] character is the heroine, but I have used the hero and it can work well.

The opening image and opening scene establish the main character in their ordinary world and creates an immediate connection between the reader and this character.

The key thing is that you have to have someone on the page who a reader, you in this case, since this first draft is for, can root for and sympathise with.

You have to like this person, whether it is the hero or the heroine, and want to spend time with them.

Show us this person in their ordinary life, then allow the character to reveal why they are feeling stressed and at the end of their tether and hint at that one limiting belief that guides their life.

Hook the reader with interesting characters. Build sympathy and empathy by showing that they are lacking something. They come onto the stage with their own needs and wants and expectations for the future.

Introduce the hero into this world.

The second scene introduces the other main character. So, if I have the heroine POV in scene one, then the hero is in scene two.

In both cases, by the end of each scene, the reader should have a good idea about who this person is and what they are doing and feeling inside this story world.

Of course, there are no fixed rules here.

Some authors like to have the heroine and hero meeting in the first few pages of the book.

Personally I would recommend establishing the heroine in the mind of the reader before you bring in the hero, so that connection is made.

This sequence ends with a Plot Point or Turning Point #1, called the **Inciting Incident**. Something unusual happens in this ordinary world which completely turns their world around.

Start of Character Arc > Resistance > Growth Transformation.

Each scene will have one character who drives the action and conflict, which leads the other character to have an emotional response and then a physical response to what has happened. They have to decide about what to do next.

The resolution of the conflict in one sequence means that a new decision was taken, which will automatically lead to the beginning of the next scene, which will lead to a new decision that will spin off to another decision.

So, each scene automatically generates a follow on scene as a reaction to the new decision.

In this segment, there could be some attraction and they fight it as being ridiculous

Both of these set-up scenes can be very short, a few pages at most, because the third element is all about getting them together on the page. Their first meeting.

The scene where our hero and heroine meet will set the tone for the rest of the romance story. It could be negative, confrontational, suspicious, or embarrassing and funny. But it should always provide the spark for the rest of the romance.

One note. Please don't fall into the trap of the "insta-lust" type of first meeting scene where you only describe how much the hero wants to see the heroine without her clothing unless you are writing that kind of erotic romance where this is the expected form for this scene.

There should be some kind of hook here beyond physical attraction. If the story situation means that the hero and heroine are competing for the same thing or are unsure of one another, then that doubt will offset any attraction just like it does in life.

Is it possible to create a "Conflict Lock" for the hero and heroine, where each person is highly motivated to achieve a certain thing –

but if they do, it will block the other person from having what they want?

This is why it is super-useful to work on the character needs for one character at the start and set it up so that the hero or heroine wants the same thing for different reasons.

When the heroine first meets the hero, she may already know who he is, or recognises him from the past when he was at high school in this small town and very much from the wrong side of the tracks. Do you see the idea?

If you are writing a novella or a very short romance novel, then this can actually be the opening scene and you go straight into the action, as seen from the POV of the hero or heroine.

In this case, the story idea will guide why these two people have been brought together in a situation that is outside of their ordinary lives.

The detailed internal beliefs will have to be woven into the scenes through dialogue or introspection later.

Act One. Sequence Two. From the Inciting Incident to the first Major Turning point at the end of Act One.

Our hero and heroine have to react to this Inciting Incident and new situation.

They don't want to change, and they are going to resist moving out of their established lives, but something pushes them to commit to change and try something new.

This is the external plot that brings the hero and heroine together and forces them to stay locked together. The romance begins!

Something happens which forces them to make a decision that will lock them together.

Do you remember that scene from the movie "Notting Hill" when Hugh Grant spills juice over Julia Roberts?

It could be as simple as the hero turns the corner on a busy street and spills juice all over the heroine. She is shocked and stunned and then angry. She met the hero in the bookshop a short while earlier and they chatted, so he is not a stranger. The hero invites her to come and change in his house which is just across the street, and she decides to accept.

Scene Step Outline for the first Act

Worked Example. Hired:Sassy Assistant

Worked example. The opening chapters of my Mills and Boon book *Hired: Sassy Assistant. [The ROMANTIC TIMES magazine Top Pick for January 2010. AND the Reviewers Choice Award for Best Harlequin Romance for 2010.]*

Chapter One.

#1. Medic Kyle Munroe is on the London Underground when he sees a woman struggling with a large parcel and offers to help.

#2. Lulu Hamilton in London on way to a book launch.

Lulu gave up her university education to take care of her father when her mother died. Now she is a part-time artist.

#3. Kyle is getting ready for the book launch with his boss Mike Baxter.

Kyle has become a star on social media with his online diary in Nepal and India and has written a book. The charity wants to make a documentary and new book about his experiences as a young medic. The advance will pay for the vaccines the clinic needs. But he is useless with paperwork.

Chapter Two

#4. Lulu is waiting for Mike when the man from the tube walks in through the 'out' door.

#5. Lulu at the book launch and press conference.

Inciting Incident. Mike Baxter wants Lulu to help Kyle write a book about the time he spent with Lulu's late mother on her last mission in Africa just before she died.

#6. Lulu's reaction to the invitation. It is painful but she is persuaded to consider it.

Chapter Three

#7. Lulu is dreading the thought of going through her mother's letters and diaries and the pain of her sudden death in Africa.

#8. Kyle explains that he needs the money for this book to buy rabies vaccines – appeals to her sense of justice. She agrees to do it.

Turning Point 1. They are locked into working together on this project.

End of Act One. Page 42/181 in the draft ~ 23%

The whole romance story kicks off from this point. No going back. The reader knows that these two people have to travel the journey together from this point.

The heroine or hero needs the other person to help them or work with them or advise them, so they are forced to talk to one another as adults. This emotional shift leads to increased attraction and awareness that the other person does have positive qualities. Being locked together changes their relationship and they have to accommodate that.

HOW TO USE NOTECARDS FOR EACH SCENE AND THE SIX-STEP PROCESS

- Use a physical or electronic bulletin board such as Pinterest. Pin up or link to inspirational photos of the locations that you found on the web or in magazines etc.

- Collect together a whole stack of index cards or a pad of sticky notes or cut in half pieces of paper. Anything that you can write a few lines on.

  This is one time when pen on paper is a much better tool than digital spreadsheets or charts.

- Use one piece of paper or card for each scene.

- Collect snippets of dialogue and write them down or record them on your cell phone. A sudden revelation about the hero's internal conflict will come to you when your brain is in story stand-by mode such as the shower, middle of the supermarket aisle or a long walk with your dog.

- Make it fast. Bullet points and one line ideas are absolutely fine.

- You are going to scribble down notes and ideas on other cards or sheets of paper as you work through the six-step process described in previous chapters.

- Give each scene card a name that makes sense to you. For example. Hugh spills orange juice all over Julia.

You could create one long column of cards for the entire Act One on a table or cork pinboard or a whiteboard or whatever flat surface you have handy, or you can break it into sequences and have two columns of scene cards/sticky notes etc., one for each sequence of scenes.

Write the Sequence number at the top of the column and the turning point at the end of the column.

In this example, there are eight scenes that make up Act One of Hired: Sassy Assistant. This book was about 55, 000 words and follows the **Eight-Sequence, Four-Act story Structure.**

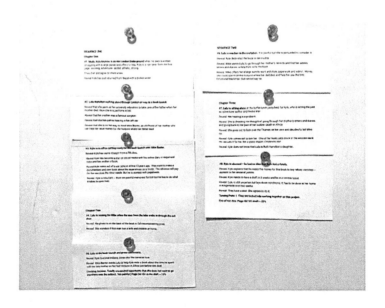

COLLECT TOGETHER YOUR NOTES

- Collect together all of your notes for Act One of your book.

- JUST Act One at this point. The goal is to work on the opening chapters and allow the character to breathe and come alive on the page, inside your storyworld.

- Stand back and take an objective view of your scenes in Act One. Ask yourself some critical questions and take notes on your cards as you go, or scribble on your printed out pages.

- Work through your notes/cards and add new cards if you come up with additional ideas about how each of the six steps. For example. Can you build on the character profile you have created for the heroine so that her limiting belief and story situation is as powerful and interesting as possible?

ORDER YOUR NOTES FOR ACT ONE

Collect together the cards for all of Act One in your story. Order them into a short outline for the opening scenes.

There should be two major events: **The Inciting Incident** at the end of the first sequence of scenes when the ordinary lives of both hero and heroine are thrown into turmoil.

And the first **Major Turning Point** where the hero and heroine make a decision that will lock them together so that they will be forced to communicate and spend serious time together one to one from this point.

Congratulations! You have plotted the opening scenes for your romance. Now you can dive into the writing.

WRITING THE FIRST DRAFT

WRITING THE OPENING SCENES

If you write in strict order, then your objective is to write from one orientation point to the next, following the hero and the heroine as they fall in love and experiencing the ups and downs, conflicts, and complications at the same time as they do.

On the other hand, I know many authors who prefer to jot down notes and write the scene as it comes to them, which could be at any point in the story.

This is often a major turning point scene where the conflicts will be exposed or a secret is revealed, making one of the characters more vulnerable than before.

Because the action in one scene leads to the reaction in the following scene, this can be a fast way to get into the story as quickly as possible.

Be prepared and give yourself full permission to write a seriously rough first draft- this WVFD (word-vomit first draft), otherwise, there is a real risk that you will lose all of your momentum in the first three chapters and never finish the first draft.

This is crucial.

If you don't know something about a detail, then you can highlight the text in Word or leave a marker or comment bubble in the text, like {{what kind of saddle does a cowboy use in a rodeo}} or {{ would her sister really sleep with her boyfriend just to prove that he is being unfaithful behind her back – work out the real motivation?}} and come back later when the manuscript is complete and you have done your research, but don't step away to track down the information or work on a character now.

You know what would happen if you went onto the internet. Two hours later you would have found another fine form of procrastination.

Drive on ahead, even if it feels incomplete.

Then you can come back after you reach the end of the stage and go through the comments and notes and fix anything that adds to the story at that point.

You are bound to have new ideas for scenes as you write, so jot them down on the last page of your document if you are on a computer or an "ideas" file. Then you can work those scenes in when you come back to the draft or discard them if they don't fit.

BUILD ON WHAT YOU HAVE LEARNT AFTER WRITING THE SCENES FOR ACT ONE.

By the end of the opening sequences of scenes, the hero and heroine are locked together in some way it is difficult to escape from, usually linked to the story situation which brought them together.

So, let's pause at this triangulation point on the route and take our bearings.

Starting at Chapter one, scene one, read your manuscript through to the end of Act One – if you know where that is, or about the 25% stage if you are unsure. You are not reading for pleasure. You are reading to get the big picture.

Some authors prefer to print out these opening chapters so that can sit down with their editor pen and mark out where scenes shift, and new scenes begin.

Review what you have written and pull out the key threads.

Now is the time to work backwards through the scenes you have already written and note down the key beliefs and fears that you want to work with.

Write down the key "beats" or action points about what happens in that scene. One point of view. One character. What they are doing. What happens in this scene? How does it move the story forwards?

- Remap the scenes. You know the endpoint of Sequence One and Sequence Two. Now you can make sure that you have built the story to support the Inciting Incident at the end of Sequence One and the main Turning point at the end of Sequence Two when the hero and heroine are locked together in some way.

- Reorganize the manuscript to create the most compelling story arc for your characters in this romance.

- Is there a great hook in the first few scenes leading to the Inciting Incident which will keep readers turning the pages?

- Ask yourself constant questions about what people are doing and why.

- How many scenes have the heroine POV?

- How many scenes are the hero's POV? Can you improve the balance so that the readers discover more about each character?

- If most of the scenes are from one POV, would it be better to rewrite them as first person POV and get deeper inside the head of that main character? Yes, I know how much work that would take but it could transform a story from good to great and you have only just started a first "discovery" draft.

- Find out now if there are missing scenes or too many scenes [save any deleted text in a separate document].

- Go back to your scene cards and move them around. Add notes to every card. Write extra cards and pin them where they should go in your scene sequence. Take out scene cards that aren't delivering and write new ones to take their place.

- Build a scene sequence outline of the new scenes you are going to write. Check that the structure delivers the emotional impact you are looking for.

- Go to each scene in your manuscript for Act One. Add your notes and ideas to the start of each scene. Reorder them if you need to, insert new scenes, and add your notes for that scene. Change the colour of the text you want to delete from black to red or some other bright colour you cannot miss.

- Start work rewriting and editing the scenes. Give this the time it needs! It can take several drafts. This is okay. This is normal.

DEVELOP TURNING POINTS FOR THE REST OF YOUR ROMANCE NOVEL

Use the Eight Sequence, Four Act, structure I described above to outline the scene sequences in the other three Acts of your romance.

The goal is to create signposts for the couple on their journey to love, in the form of story turning points at the end of each of the eight sequences of scenes.

At each turning point, there will be a shift in both the external and emotional storyline, that forces the hero and heroine to pivot and make new decisions, propelling the story forwards.

If it helps, create separate documents for each Act so that you don't feel overwhelmed.

Options. Some authors go straight to Act Four and work on the end of the character arc you have just created in Act One for your hero and heroine and that's fine. You do whatever works for you. This is your book and your process.

Yes. You will be moving scenes, adding conflict and detail so you should expect to have to come back to the opening chapters to create the starting point for those changes, but you are doing so from a strong opening structure.

Don't worry if these are just woolly ideas at this point. They are meant to be guides, not fixed monuments.

The good news?

Once you understand the Four-Act, Eight-Sequence Story Structure and can apply it to your work, you can apply it for your next book and the book after that. Building powerful stories that readers will love and your career as a fiction author.

DECONSTRUCTION OF THE PLOT OF A PUBLISHED ROMANCE NOVEL

DECONSTRUCTION OF HIRED: SASSY ASSISTANT

The life of a reclusive artist changes when she meets a famous adventurer and dedicated doctor.

Hired: Sassy Assistant was The ROMANTIC TIMES magazine Top Pick for January 2010. AND the Reviewers Choice Award for Best Harlequin Romance for 2010.

Theme = Reverse Cinderella story. Lulu Hamilton is Cinderella. Kyle Munroe is the prince. Kyle as the prince falls for Cinderella Lulu and she rescues him and herself.

Where? Establish location. The London Underground and the South Bank art galleries where Lulu is selling her work.

Who? Lulu Hamilton is the main protagonist. Her journey will be followed in this story.

Chapter One.

Medic Kyle Munroe is on the London Underground when he sees a woman struggling with a large parcel and offers to help. Kyle is a risk-taker from the first page: exciting, adventurer, skilled, athletic, strong. They chat and share witty banter and agree to share a taxi.

Reveal that Kyle has just returned from Nepal with a broken wrist.

Lulu Hamilton in London on way to a book launch.

Reveal that she gave up her university education to take care of her father when her mother died. Now she is a part-time artist.

Reveal that her mother was a famous surgeon.

Reveal that she has partial hearing.

Reveal that she is on her way to meet Mike Baxter, an old friend of her mother who can help her raise money for the hospice where her father died.

Kyle is in an office getting ready for the book launch with Mike Baxter.

Reveal that Kyle has come straight from a TB clinic.

Reveal that Kyle has become a star on social media with his online diary in Nepal and India and has written a book.

Reveal that Kyle came out of a war zone in Africa 10 years ago.

They want to make a documentary and a new book about his experiences as a medic. The advance will pay for the vaccines the clinic needs. But he is useless with paperwork.

Reveal. Kyle is reluctant – there are painful memories for him, but he has to do what it takes to save lives. He agrees to work on the project.

> **ACT ONE PINCH POINT. Something happens linked to the inciting incident which forces the protagonist to make a decision and do something different.**

> **ACT ONE. SEQUENCE TWO**

Chapter Two

 # Lulu is waiting for Mike when the man from the tube walks in through the out door.

Reveal. His photo is on the back of the book in a mountaineering pose.

Reveal. She wonders if this man has a wife and children at home.

 # Lulu at the book launch and press conference.

Reveal. Kyle is a total Indiana Jones star the cameras love.

Reveal. Mike Baxter wants Lulu to help Kyle write a book about the time he spent with her late mother on her last mission in Africa just before she died.

> **INCITING INCIDENT. Totally unexpected opportunity that she does not want to go anywhere near the subject. Too painful. Opposite of Good news but leads to the heroine's happiness. Page 24/181 in the draft ~ 13%**

 # Lulu's reaction to the invitation. It is painful but she is persuaded to consider it.

Reveal. Kyle dedicated the book to her mother.

Reveal. Mike wants Lulu to go through her mother's records and find her weekly letters and diaries to help Kyle write the book.

Reveal. Mike offers her a large sum to work with Kyle, paperwork, and admin. Money she could spend on the hospice where her dad died and help her pay the bills. Emotional blackmail. But cannot say no.

Chapter Three

Lulu is sitting alone at the buffet lunch party held for Kyle, who is acting the part as adventurer author and media star.

Reveal. Her hearing is a problem.

Reveal. She is dreading the thought of going through her mother's letters and diaries and going back to the pain of her sudden death in Africa.

Reveal. She goes out to look over the Thames on her own and decides to tell Mike no.

Kyle is stunned – he had no idea that Ruth had a family.

Reveal. Kyle explains that he needs the money for this book to buy rabies vaccines – appeals to her sense of justice.

Reveal. Kyle needs to have a draft in 3 weeks, and he is a terrible typist.

Reveal. Lulu is still uncertain but lays down conditions. It has to be done at her home in Kingsmede over two weeks.

Reveal. They have a deal. She agrees to do it.

Turning Point 1. They are locked into working together on this project. End of Act One. Page 42/181 in the draft ~ 23%

> **END OF ACT ONE LOCKING EVENT. MAJOR TURNING POINT ONE.**
>
> This is the crucial scene where the main character leaves his ordinary world and sets out to discover a new land on a quest to find, in a romantic comedy, love. **Now you must deliver on the promise you have made to your target audience. WE SHIFT INTO ACT TWO. SEQUENCE THREE.**

> **ACT TWO. SEQUENCE THREE.**
>
> Act Two is the point when the love story really begins and the excitement and thrill of falling in love challenges both of the characters. Imagine that you are filming a trailer for your story – most of the clips would come from these scenes.

Chapter Four

Kyle comes to Lulu's House

Lulu has laid out the boxes of records from the African clinic where Kyle and her mother had worked for the Medical Foundation.

Reveal. Lulu has read Kyle's book which is filled with humour, charm, and hard work.

Reveal. Lulu lost her hearing because of an infection she caught in Africa.

Kyle arrives at the house

Kyle is still recovering from serious chest infections as well as his broken arm. He needs this break away from the clinic.

Coming to this house reminds him of the last time he saw Lulu's mother ten years ago before her ambulance was blown up by a land mine.

He arrives to find Lulu playing with her dog and is stunned.

> **RELATIONSHIP DEVELOPS. FUN AND GAMES**

Chapter Five

#. Lulu shows Kyle around the brightly coloured house and tells him about her late father, Tom Hamilton, who was a professional artist.

#. Kyle asks Lulu to work with him on the book.

 # Lulu agrees – she is a typist and the sooner it is done the sooner she can get paid and get her home back.

#When Kyle starts coughing and asks for directions to the nearest hotel, Lulu surprises herself by asking him if he would like to stay at her house.

> **THIS PINCH POINT DEMONSTRATES A CHANGE IN THEIR RELATIONSHIP IN RESPONSE TO CHALLENGES. They are locked into working together on this project. Page 74/181 in the draft ~ 40%**

Chapter Six

 # Kyle is surprised but Lulu convinces him to stay.

In the process, they both reveal that they are single.

 # Reveal. Kyle is holding back. He should have been in that ambulance that morning when Lulu's mother diverted onto a road set with landmines to avoid an army convoy. He has always blamed himself.

#**Reveal. He finds Lulu very** attractive but agrees to stay.

ACT TWO. SEQUENCE FOUR- REACTION TO THE CHALLENGE

Next morning Kyle is awake before Lulu

Reveal. Lulu's dog already adored him.

Reveal. He had relied on Lulu's mother and the team to help him.

Reveal. Lulu had not read her mother's letters and does not really want to read her diaries, even for the book.

Reveal. Kyle shares his memories of her mother and the cases they worked on.

Chapter Seven

Kyle and Lulu walk back from the pub where Kyle had been given a real village welcome, complete with banners and photographers.

Reveal that Lulu loves painting.

Lulu's dog goes into the river after ducks and is being swept away by the current.

Kyle wades into the icy water fully clothed and hoists the dog into his shoulders.

Back at the house, Lulu gives Kyle a brilliant idea about how to collect the material for his book and he kisses her on the cheek before she helps him strip out of his wet clothing.

#Lulu tells Kyle how the house had become a refuge for any passing medic or refugee family desperate for somewhere safe to stay. Most of them headed for the nearest hospital. But it got too much, and she walked out and went to her godmother's cottage in the village. She came every day to check there was food and the bills were paid. Then she went to art school.

She came home when her mother died. It is too painful for her to talk about.

Kyle's hand was on her waist, the gentle pressure turning her towards him and closer, ever closer, so that they were looking at one other on the sofa, their faces only inches apart. His hand moved to her cheek, his thumb on her jaw, as his eyes scanned her face, back and forth.

'Don't lock me out. Please.' His voice was low, steady. 'Trust me Lulu. Can you do that? Trust me?'

Chapter Six

Kyle reveals his messy family story.

His mother has had several strokes and his parents are divorced.

When Lulu responds warmly, Kyle kisses her.

> **Turning Point 3 is at about the halfway point through the SCRIPT. This is also known as the Midpoint of No Return. They cannot go back from this point.**
>
> This could be a sexual, close, intimate, or personal moment, but it has to be a fundamental shift in their relationship that changes the entire direction of the story. **Page 118/181 in the draft ~ 65%**

ACT THREE. SEQUENCE FIVE

Lulu and Kyle bond over the work and laughter.

Lulu tells Kyle about how she came to lose her hearing.

#They become more intimate and their contact turns to passion.

> **SHIFT INTO ACT THREE. SEQUENCE SIX. STAKES AND PROBLEMS RAMP UP. Page 126/181 in the draft 70%**

Chapter Nine

#They are interrupted by Lulu's godmother who chats with Lulu and then Kyle. Lulu is holding her birthday party at the house.

Reality bites home. Lulu knows that Kyle will be going back overseas soon. Her parents had loved one another but it was not enough to make her mother stay so she abandoned her husband and her daughter.

#Kyle realises that he is infatuated with Lulu. They sit down together and work through the boxes of photographs to select some for the book.

Kyle admits that it is hard to leave the people he loves behind. It does not have to be that way with Lulu. He asks her to come to meet his family in London.

> **INTENSIFICATION**. Raising the Stakes. The protagonist s journey starts to get considerably tougher. The tempo increases. The protagonist s drive increases to match the increasing conflict.
>
> **Page 141/181 in the draft ~ 78%**

Chapter Ten

 # It is the birthday party and Kyle and Lulu are happy and laughing. Kyle feels that he has been made part of this warm, close community.

 # Kyle realizes that he is in love with Lulu who is dressed in a sari with gold jewellery and looks stunning.

 # Kyle pulls her to one side to have a private and intimate dance before the local children drag Kyle away to find Lulu's dog that had run away.

#After the party Lulu is alone with Kyle and knows that she loves him, even though she is setting herself up for pain and loneliness.

#Kyle tells Lulu that there is something he needs to tell her. He is leaving in the morning. And he was the last person to see her mother alive.

Chapter Eleven

#Kyle confesses that he is the one who should have died in the ambulance that day. Her mother took his shift because he was too exhausted.

#Lulu tells him to leave, and he drives away, leaving her bereft with her dog.

> **Sequence 6 ends with Turning Point#4, Major Setback, at about the 75% point through the book.**
>
> This is also known as the Dark Night of the Soul or the Black Moment and is a compulsory plot point in any romance. **Page 164/181 in the draft ~ 90%**

ACT FOUR. SEQUENCE SEVEN.

#Lulu has to work on her paintings and suddenly realises that she is holding back – now she is going to paint what she wants.

 # Lulu finds a letter from her mother that her dad has kept in his sketchbook which explained the relationship and how much her mother had loved them, safe at home in England. *If you love someone, let them go.*

 # Lulu has to risk everything and tell Kyle how she feels or regret it for the rest of her life.

Sequence Seven ends in Turning Point#5. The Climax decision. Do or die. Commit, compromise or walk away. Usually at the 90% point.

Chapter Twelve

#Lulu jumps on her old cycle and pedals hard – terrified that Kyle had already left.

#Lulu and Kyle talk.

'You love me, but you are willing to let me go and do the work which means so much to me? Is that right?'

ACT FOUR. SEQUENCE EIGHT

SELF-REVELATION FROM ONE OF THE CHARACTERS LEADING TO RECONCILIATION.

<u>**SELF-REVELATION**</u>

#Kyle feels the same. *'What would you say if I told you that I would be working out of London for the next twelve months?'* He has changed everything so that he can work on fundraising in London and be with Lulu. As his wife.

RESOLUTION AND DENOUMENT.

Final image. Opposite to opening image. Bookends.

#Kyle and Lulu splashing in the river together, dancing and laughing before collapsing into a passionate kiss.

#Epilogue. Kyle and Lulu are married and celebrating her latest art exhibition. Kyle has been promoted and travelling all over Africa and India with Lulu.

SUMMARY

ACCEPT YOUR WRITING PROCESS AND INCLUDE AN EARLY PLANNING STAGE

Architects generate plans before the builders start ordering the bricks.

They know that they are expected to design a two-storey modern house, not a car park or supermarket or farm building.

They have expectations about the form of building that they are looking for and what that building has to contain.

Musicians use musical forms so that when they create a sonata or a symphony they use the same sound patterns perfected by the great masters.

There are some authors who have assimilated decades of reading and writing practice to create an ideal "form" for a story inside their head, and they can use this to instinctively recognise the pattern of the story beats before they even start to write. Then they spend serious amounts of time editing and revising that first draft.

Other writers love to free write as part of the story development process and that is key to bringing them the best from their characters.

They are happy to write a first draft that has twice the target wordcount that they need and more characters than the bible, because they know that they will explore all of the possible side alleys the characters have walked down on the journey in that draft.

I hope that this book has demonstrated that there is a middle ground and provided you with ideas on how you can include a six-step story development process to create a compelling romance that matches your vision and sparks your creativity - without having to plot out the entire novel.

I wish you all the best in your writing!

Nina

THANK YOU

Before you go, I hope that you enjoyed this copy of: How to Plot Romance Fiction.

If you did, please help other readers find this book by writing a review of this book for the bookstore where you purchased it. It would be greatly appreciated.

As a way of saying thank you for purchasing this book, I am offering a **Free Story Planning Video Course with the key Master Story Maps you need to Outline Your Romance Novel – Fast!**

To Find Out More and Receive Your Free Video Training Course go to: https://www.subscribepage.com/HOWTOPLOTROMANCE FICTION

ABOUT THE AUTHOR

Nina Harrington grew up in rural Northumberland, England, and decided aged eleven that her dream job was to be a librarian because then she could read all of the books in the public library whenever she wanted!

Many years later she took the bold decision to take a career break from working in the pharmaceutical industry to realise her dream of being a fiction writer. No contract, no cash, but a compelling passion for the written word.

Nina writes fun, award winning contemporary romance for the Mills and Boon Modern Tempted / Harlequin KISS lines, single title romantic mysteries, and guides and training courses for authors.

Over 1.7 million of her books have been sold in 28 countries and translated into 23 languages.

When she is not creating stories which make her readers smile, or researching best practices for prolific authors, her hobbies are cooking, eating, enjoying good wine, and talking, for which she has had specialist training.

Find out more about Nina at: http://www.ninaharrington.com.

Printed in Great Britain
by Amazon

77759325R00058